Girls Bravo vol. 3
Created by Mario Kaneda

Translation - Asuka Yoshizu
English Adaptation - Steve Bunche
Associate Editor - Hope Donovan
Retouch and Lettering - Erika Terriquez
Production Artist - Lucas Rivera
Cover Design - Jorge Negrete

Editor - Rob Tokar
Digital Imaging Manager - Chris Buford
Production Manager - Jennifer Miller
Managing Editor - Lindsey Johnston
VP of Production - Ron Klamert
Publisher and E.I.C. - Mike Kiley
President and C.O.O. - John Parker
C.E.O. and Chief Creative Officer - Stuart Levy

A  Manga

TOKYOPOP Inc.
5900 Wilshire Blvd. Suite 2000
Los Angeles, CA 90036

E-mail: info@TOKYOPOP.com
Come visit us online at www.TOKYOPOP.com

ISBN: 1-59816-042-7

First TOKYOPOP printing: March 2006

10 9 8 7 6 5 4 3 2 1

Printed in Canada

GIRLS BRAVO

Volume 3

By Mario Kaneda

HAMBURG // LONDON // LOS ANGELES // TOKYO

GIRLS BRAVO

Story so far

Yukinari Sasaki

Yukinari Sasaki is a young high school student with some serious girl troubles. With below-average grades and below-average height, Yukiari has been bullied and mistreated by women his entire life. As a result, he's developed a unique female-phobia and can't touch any girl without breaking out in hives.

Even at home, where he should be safe, Yukinari is often tormented by his next-door neighbor Kirie Kojima. Kirie is a girl with a secret crush on Yukinari and no clue how to express herself without causing those around her bodily harm. Recently, Yukinari accidentally walked in on Kirie while she was bathing, and the nubile, nude neighbor pummeled poor Yukinari and knocked him into the bathtub. When Yukinari surfaced, he found himself in another bath with another girl on another world!

Miharu

The other bath belonged to Miharu, a beautiful, gentle, easy-going alien girl. To Yukinari's surprise, Miharu didn't make him break out in hives, even after their close physical contact. The other world was Siren--a serene planet with blue trees. To Yukinari's horror, Siren's population is 90% female.

To make matters worse for our female-phobic friend, most Siren women are so desperate for a man that Yukinari was considered an amazing catch. While Yukinari ran from Miharu's sister Maharu and a throng of horny alien women of all ages, Miharu tried to protect the earthling from the estrogen-infused onslaught. Cornered in the bathroom, the two fell into Miharu's tub...and surfaced back on Earth with Kirie.

Kirie Kojima

Yukinari was only too glad to let Miharu stay with him, as she's the first girl he's met who doesn't give him hives. She may be eating him out of house and home, but Yukinari's touched by her presence and overjoyed that she's promised to help him to overcome his female-phobia. Even Kirie has become friendlier since Miharu's appearance, though Yukinari's bumbling still occasionally stirs Kirie's killer instincts.

Kazuharu Fukuyama

It's hard to hide a girl like Miharu, and she quickly became the obsession of the wealthy, egotistical, high school playboy Kazuhara Fukuyama, a boy who's made a career out of insulting "Chibinari." Clueless as to why Miharu would chose a shrimp like Yukinari over a fine specimen like himself, Fukuyama's attempts to woo Miharu accidentally led Yukinari to discover Fukuyama's weakness: a male-allergy so severe that he can't bear even the slightest touch of another guy.

More trouble from the Fukuyama family came from Kazuhara's occult-obsessed little sister, Risa. Due to some dubious dictates from Risa's favorite occult radio host, Risa came to believe that Yukinari is the man of her destiny. When she found Yukinari already "taken" by Miharu--and allergic to all other girls--Risa made it her personal mission to cure Yukinari of his illness--and of Miharu--though her methods range from questionable to downright outrageous.

Risa Fukuyama

It didn't take long for Miharu's presence to completely change Yukinari's life. Though Yukinari's parents are out of town indefinitely, he has Miharu and Kirie as almost constant companions. Yukinari has enjoyed himself, hung out at the pool, accidentally switched bodies with Fukuyama, switched back again, and saved his school from overflowing with hundreds of drunken copies of Miharu (too much alcohol can do that to an alien gal!) Best of all, when he's with Miharu, Yukinari is hive-free.

Just when the abnormal almost started seeming routine, Koyomi, a pretty young agent from Siren, showed up to take Miharu back to their homeworld. Possibly as a result of living on a planet with such a lopsided gender balance (or possibly as a result of being a naturally timid person), Koyomi has a strong male-phobia that usually drives her to hide from domineering men-folk. Entering the chaos that is present every day in Yukinari's home, Koyomi was so freaked out that she dug a hole through the floor to hide. However, after Koyomi and Miharu cleared a few things up on Siren, Miharu was granted leave to stay on Earth indefinitely, and Koyomi returned with her. Can a beautiful, shy, male-phobic girl survive in a world full of desperate men?

Koyomi

Act. 13
HMM...
THIS ONE!
JOKER
SHE GETS SO EXCITED JUST PLAYING OLD MAID... SOMETIMES MIHARU IS JUST TOO CUTE.
OH, YEAH! I DID IT! I BEAT YOU, YUKINARI! ♡

GIRLS BRAVO
MARIO KANEDA
まりお金田
3

GIRLS BRAVO 3

CONTENTS

ACT 13 007

ACT 14 035

ACT 15 059

ACT 16 087

ACT 17 111

ACT 18 135

ACT 19 159

THESE CARD GAMES ARE A LOT OF FUN!
WE HAVE SIMILAR GAMES IN SIREN, TOO.
THAT'S GREAT...BUT IT'S MORE FUN TO PLAY CARDS WITH FOUR OR FIVE PEOPLE.
GAMES FINISH TOO QUICKLY WHEN ONLY TWO PEOPLE ARE PLAYING...
HEY! WHY DON'T WE INVITE KIRIE?
GOOD IDEA!
WE CAN ALL PLAY TOGETHER!!

SO TELL ME...
WHAT ARE YOU DOING HERE?!
This house is crowded, as usual...
BECAUSE...
MIHARU INVITED ME!
Ahem!
WHY DID YOU INVITE THIS JERK?
MIHARU!
...YUKINARI TOLD ME IT'S MORE FUN TO PLAY CARDS WITH A GROUP...
YOU IDIOT, YUKI-NARI!!
HOW WOULD I KNOW SHE'D INVITE FUKU-YAMA?
?

AH.
I WAS INVITED TO "PLAY GAMES TOGETHER"...
Hmm...
AND I SEE... CARDS...
FUKUYAMA... DON'T YOU LIKE TO PLAY CARDS?
MIHARU...
...WHY DON'T WE PLAY SOMETHING MUCH MORE FUN THAN CARDS?!

BEHOLD!!

Take off lothes

Hug

Tops

WHA...?

!!!

THIS...
...ISN'T MAHJONG!
WHAT ARE YOU TALKING ABOUT?!
HERE... CHECK THIS OUT.
SOMETHING'S ODD.
Rub
Bell
Take off clothes
Bunny ears
Kitty ears
DIDN'T I TELL YOU THIS WASN'T MAHJONG?
WHAT IS THIS ...?
YOU CALL THIS A GAME?
OH, YEAH!!
YOU COLLECT THREE PIECES WITH EACH MOVE UNTIL YOU HAVE A SET OF TWELVE PIECES.
YOU WIN WHEN YOUR SET IS COMPLETE!
Take off clothes
Take off clothes
Take off clothes
Take off clothes
Under wear
wear

LET ME ASK YOU SOME-THING...
WHAT HAPPENS WHEN YOU WIN?
THAT ALL DEPENDS ON THE PIECES THAT YOU'VE COLLECT-ED!
We write down the player's names on those blank pieces!!
CHIBINARI... TOWEL...
THROW ME A TOWEL...
I DON'T HAVE A TOWEL. MAN, YOU'RE A PAIN...
IT SOUNDS LIKE A FUN GAME!
BACK IN SIREN, WE ALSO HAVE A GAME WHERE WE TAKE OFF CLOTHES WHEN WE LOSE.
IN SIREN...?

Note: Strip "Rock-Paper-Scissors" is known as "Yakyu-ken" in Japan.

SHE'S RIGHT, CHIBINARI!
AND WHAT ARE YOU SO WORRIED ABOUT? WITH THREE AGAINST ONE, YOU SHOULD HAVE NO TROUBLE BEATING ME, RIGHT?
YOU CAN'T DARE US INTO PLAYING!
RIGHT, YUKI-NARI?!
Right?
UH, YEAH.
HMPH ...
WELL... IT'S A CINCH FOR ME TO GET KOJIMA BUCK-NAKED WITH MY INCREDIBLE PLAYING SKILLS...
Noooo!!
I DON'T BLAME YOU FOR BEING TOO CHICKEN TO PLAY ME!
I'm talkin' birthday suit!
WHA...
WHAT ARE YOU SAYING?!

WHO CARES ABOUT SUCH A STUPID GAME?!

WHEN I'M THROUGH, YOU'LL BE WEARING A BUNNY OUTFIT AND STRIKING A POSE, PLAYBOY STYLE!

RIGHT, YUKINARI?!

Boing

Kitty ears

Take off clothes

KIRIE...

No...

Aw...

HEH HEH HEH...

SO, IT'S A DEAL. THEN...

THANKS TO KIRIE WE'RE STUCK PLAYING THIS SLEAZY GAME...
I HOPE THIS ENDS BEFORE THINGS GET TOO RAUNCHY...
じゃら
じゃら

...BUT THINGS LOOK BAD ALREADY. HE'S REALLY GETTING INTO IT...
Any way you cut it, this is ...no good!!

Round One

HA HA. I'M GETTING SOME GOOD PIECES. ♡

You just wait, Fukuyama!!

OH!

THAT'S...

...A WIN FOR ME.

YOU'RE CHEATING OR SOMETHING, AREN'T YOU?!
THAT'S TOO SOON! IT'S FISHY!
WELL, WE CAN QUIT NOW IF YOU DON'T LIKE IT.
BUT YOU STILL HAVE TO TAKE OFF YOUR TOP, SINCE YOU LOST!!
CAN YOU PROVE I CHEATED?
GRR...
YOU SAYING I'M A QUITTER?!
Boing ♥
Meet "the Twins"!
YEESH!
NEXT!
LET'S GO!!
Grrr... I should have put on more clothes!

Round Two

OH!

I GOT LUCKY!

Put on clothes

Put on clothes

Put on clothes

Apron

Apron

LET'S SEE...

"KOJIMA." "PUT ON CLOTHES."

"APRON" AND "KITTY EARS"!!

M-ME, ***AGAIN?!***

Noooo!!

I can't handle seeing you in that bra...

Kojima

BUT, LOOK... IT SAYS, "PUT ON CLOTHES," SO IT'S BY THE RULES. ISN'T THAT GOOD?

ぷるっ……

....

HE... HEY...
ISN'T THIS...
THIS LOOKS LIKE...
Wow! That's great!
WOW! YOU LOOK LIKE A SEXY KITTY CAT!
THAT'S THE LAST THING I NEED IN MY HEAD!!
YOU'LL START A NEW CRAZE WITH THOSE KITTY EARS, KOJIMA!!
Ha ha ha!
UGH!
AARGH! YUKINARI, YOU IDIOT!!
WHAT WAS THAT FOR?!
I did her a favor!!

After things cooled off,
Round Three
YEAH!
I WON!
Take off clothes
Chibinari
Chibinari
Chibinari
"CHIBINARI." "TAKE OFF CLOTHES."
"TWO" AND "BUNNY EARS."
Crap!
AW...
MIHARU, HOW COULD YOU DO THIS TO ME?
CHIBINARI! GET OUT OF THAT LUDICROUS OUTFIT! YOU'RE EMBARRASSING YOURSELF!
YOU'RE THE ONE WHO *BROUGHT* THIS STUFF!!
Puke
You're embarrassing yourself!!

Round Four

OH.

I WIN AGAIN!

Take off clothes

Take off clothes

Take off clothes

Miharu

LET ME SEE...

THIS TIME...

"MIHARU." "TAKE OFF CLOTHES."

"TWO" AND "BELL."

OH... THAT'S RIGHT...

I WAS SO PSYCHED ABOUT WINNING...

SORRY ABOUT THAT.

I'll be careful from now on.

THIS CAN'T BE GOOD...

OH, MIHARU!

ANY-WAY!

LET'S KEEP PLAYING!

I just know I'll win!

WELL, MIHARU, I'M IMPRESSED!

NOW IT'S TIME FOR ME TO GET SERIOUS!!

HA HA HA HA!
Round Five
NOW!!
TAKE OFF YOUR CLOTHES!!
First Set
Take off clothes
TAKE THEM OFF!!
Second Set
NO MORE HOLDING BACK!!! NO MODESTY!!!
EEEEEK!
TAKE IT ALL OFF!!
Third Set

I CAN'T...

ぶる

ぶる

I CAN'T DO THIS...

OHH! KIRIE'S STUCK IN THAT PROVOCATIVE COSTUME...

...WHICH SHE'D NEVER IN HER LIFE THINK OF WEARING...

AND IT'S PARTLY YOUR FAULT!!

I'M SORRY!!!

KOJIMA'S LOSING IT...
JUST A LITTLE FURTHER!
OH, BOY... IF THIS KEEPS UP...
...KIRIE AND MIHARU WILL BE IN FOR IT.
IF ONE PLAYER LOSES WHEN THEY TAKE OFF ALL OF THEIR CLOTHES...
...WHY ARE THERE PIECES FOR PUTTING ON CLOTHES? WEIRD...
BLAME THE GUY WHO BROUGHT THE GAME.
HEY...
FUKUYAMA.
HUH?
LET'S MAKE THE NEXT ROUND THE LAST ONE...
...AND HAVE THE LOSER PARADE AROUND THE NEIGHBORHOOD IN THEIR COSTUME. WHAT DO YOU SAY?
What?!

GOOD IDEA. THIS GAME WILL NEVER END IF IT KEEPS GOING LIKE THIS.

I LIKE THE SOUND OF THAT!

HEY...

KIRIE, WHAT THE HECK ARE YOU TALKING--

WAIT A SEC!!

THEY'VE ALL GONE NUTS!

Rub
ERR...
I'LL TAKE THE NEXT PIECE...
Sea shell
YUKINARI?! WHAT ARE YOU THINKING?! ANSWER CAREFULLY OR I'LL KICK YOUR BUTT!!
Kick your butt and walk out!
AHHHH!!
I can't give away my strategy.
OF ALL THE OUTFITS TO CHOOSE FROM, I GET THIS ONE?!
No way am I gonna wear this!
KOJIMA.
DON'T GET SO MAD! IT'S JUST A GAME, ISN'T IT?
Heh heh.

THIS ISN'T A GAME AT ALL!!

PUTTING ON THESE WEIRD COSTUMES IS NOT MY IDEA OF FUN!

I'M RATHER ENJOYING IT.

NOW IT'S WAR!

HUH...

Bunny ears

Kitty ears

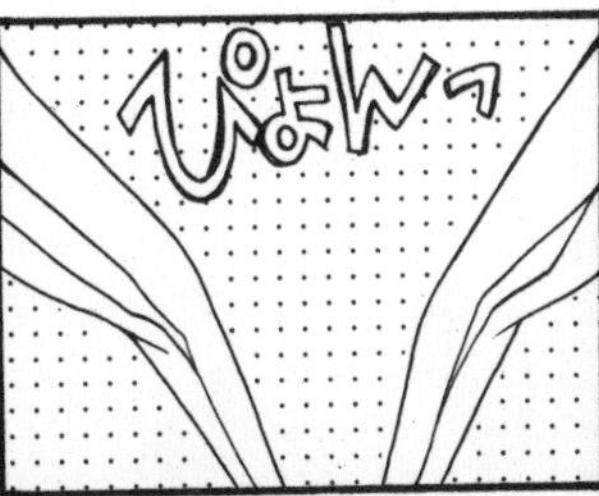

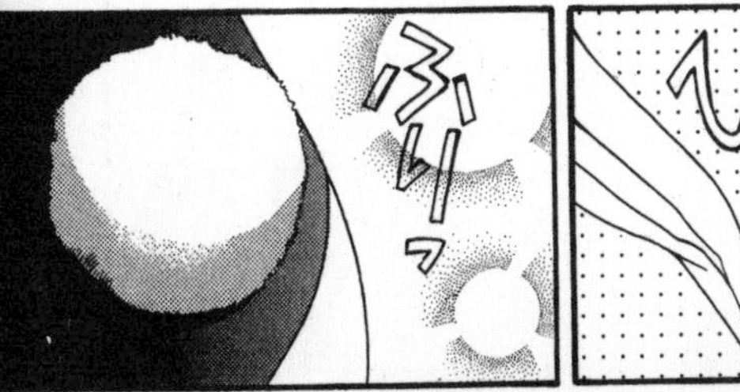

HMM...
KAZUHARU
GO BACK TO HEF'S MANSION!
HEY, I LOOK PRETTY HOT IN A BUNNY COSTUME!!
Right?
What the?
Oh my! Beefcake!!

ct.13 • END

Act.14

SIGH.

MY SECOND MISSION ON EARTH...

Requested by: MaHaru Sena Kanaka
Search for: My Husband♡♡
Assigned to: Koyomi Hare

NO DeaDLine, JUSt bring me a man! ASAP!!!

びーしっ

THIS IS SOME JOB...

Hmm...

CAN I HANDLE IT...?

HEY, KOYOMI...
YOU ALL RIGHT?
Act. 14

YES...
I'VE STUDIED UP ON THE EARTH. I'LL BE FINE.

WE'D LOVE TO STAY AND CHAT...
...BUT WE HAVE TO GO TO SCHOOL. I'M SORRY.

OH...DON'T APOLOGIZE... I'M WORKING ANYWAY.

Oh, hi Kirie!
YUKINARI! GET A MOVE ON.
WE'LL BE LATE FOR SCHOOL AGAIN!

OH, IS IT THAT LATE ALREADY?
HEY! RISA DIDN'T SHOW UP TODAY.

OH, YEAH...
SHE HASN'T SHOWN UP LATELY...
THAT'S RIGHT...
WHAT'S HAPPENED TO RISA?
WHY? DO YOU MISS HER?
NO! IT'S NOT THAT!

ERR...

WHO'S RISA?

OH.
KOYOMI HASN'T MET HER YET.

RISA GOES TO OUR SCHOOL...
She's a nice girl, I think, but...a bit weird.
HUNH.

WELL, AS LONG AS YOU'RE HERE, YOU'LL SEE HER EVEN-TUALLY.
YOU'RE BETTER OFF NOT SEEING HER AT ALL.
Ha ha.
Sigh...

I SEE.
SHE SOUNDS INTERESTING.

SEE YA.
LATER, KOYOMI!!
GOOD LUCK!

...BUT I DIDN'T EXPECT A NEW RIVAL!!

ARGH!!!
I CAN'T JUST SIT AROUND LIKE THIS!!
HAYATE! KOSAME!
APPEAR!
GO KEEP AN EYE ON THAT GIRL.
HOW MAY WE HELP YOU, MILADY?
AS YOU WISH.
AH!
What's that?
OH!

......
ALTHOUGH I HAVE TO FIND A MAN TO BE MAHARU'S BOYFRIEND...
...I'VE NEVER TALKED MUCH TO MEN.
I HAVE NO IDEA HOW TO GO ABOUT THIS.
BUT WITHOUT GAINING POINTS I CAN'T GET PROMOTED.
What did you say? How rude!!
AND WITHOUT MY HELP, POOR MAHARU HAS NO CHANCE OF GETTING MARRIED!!
I MUST DO MY BEST!

ERR...
EXCUSE ME.
YES...
UH?
HUH?!
I SWEAR I JUST HEARD SOMEONE.
AM I HEARING THINGS?!
AH... AH...
Weird...

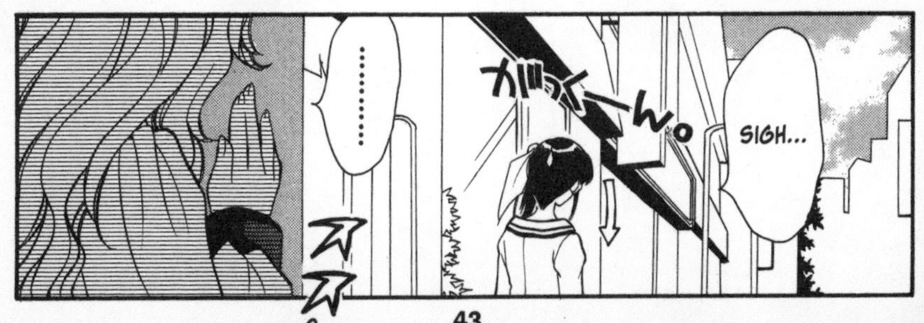

HAYATE...
KOSAME...
WHAT'S THAT GIRL DOING?

ACCORDING TO THE INTELLIGENCE THAT WE'VE COLLECTED...
...SHE SEEMS TO BE "MALE-PHOBIC."

MALE...

...PHOBIC?

YET SHE DOESN'T SEEM TO BE AFRAID OF YUKINARI.
......
I SEE...

I GET YOU.
Grin
IN THAT CASE...

LET'S...
...TARGET HER WEAKNESS...
...MERCILESSLY!!
Ha ha ha!
ROGER.
Pi
Pi
HA HA HA HA! ♡

Sigh...

EXCUSE ME...

WAS IT YOU WHO SENT ME AN EMAIL?
?!
!!
NO... NO...
...NOT ME...
I GOT AN EMAIL, TOO!
YOU'RE SO CUTE.
TELL ME YOUR NAME.
WILL YOU REALLY BE MY GIRLFRIEND?
!!
I READ YOUR EMAIL. LET'S BE FRIENDS.
ARE YOU A STUDENT?

YAAAAAAA!!!
EEEEEEP
OH... ERR...

huff

huff

WHAT'S HAPPENING?

I DIDN'T SAY ANYTHING TO THOSE GUYS...

へたー

THERE SHE IS!

THAT'S THE GIRL WITH THE WHITE RIBBON!

I FINALLY FOUND YOU! WON'T YOU GO OUT WITH ME?

SUFFER! TASTE FEAR!!
AND LEAVE YUKINARI'S HOUSE SOON!
Ha ha ha ha ha!
GOOD.
THIS SHOULD BE FINE.
YES.
Please Marry Me
I'm a bit goofy, but I'm looking for a gentle husband!
WOW!!
SHE'S HOT!
OH.
?
OH.

WOOF!! SHE'S DAINTY!!!
SHE IS INCREDIBLY TASTY!!
HUH?
UM?
WHAT DO YOU WANT?!
OH...
I'M SORRY ...
?!
Marry me!
LET'S DO IT!
LET'S DO IT RIGHT NOW!!
I'LL DUMP MY WIFE AND KIDS!
pant
pant
DO... WHAT...?
IS VEGAS OKAY FOR OUR HONEY-MOON?!
PLEASE DON'T LEAVE THEM...
What is he talking about?!
WHERE'S VEGAS?
I...
HEY, WAIT!
I CAN'T TAKE THIS ANY LONGER...
PLEASE... SOMEBODY... HELP ME!

ひょこっ

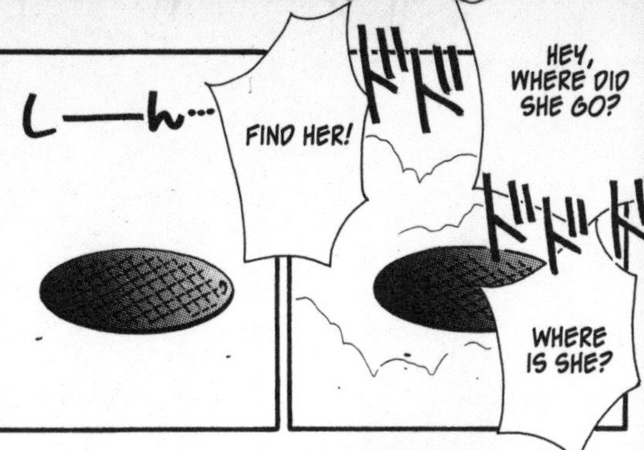
しーん…
HEY, WHERE DID SHE GO?
FIND HER!
WHERE IS SHE?

OOH...
GOOD THING THIS ARMORED HOLE WAS HERE.

THE MEN OF EARTH ARE TOO AGGRESSIVE...

FWA HA HA!
SHE'S TOTALLY STRESSED OUT! IT'S WORKING LIKE A CHARM!
くす♥

SHE'S PRETTY BUMMED OUT...

HUM...

IS THE SPELL TOO STRONG?

She's so hexed that she's even attracting spirits.

BUT THERE'S NO OTHER WAY TO GET HER OUT OF YUKINARI'S HOUSE.
Right?
Right?
ISN'T IT SO...
...MADAM MABANYA?!
HA!
MILADY RISA...

WE'VE DONE SOME MORE RESEARCH...
...AND WE FOUND THAT SHE'S LOOKING FOR A "BOYFRIEND."
WHAT?!
SO, HOW ABOUT THIS...

WE COULD INTRODUCE HER TO A POTENTIAL BOYFRIEND.
IT MIGHT BE A MORE CHARITABLE SOLUTION...
....
Hmmm...

I GUESS SO.
IF SHE HAS A BOYFRIEND, SHE WON'T MESS WITH YUKINARI.

HEY, GIRL OVER THERE!!
?!

OH... GOOD... IT'S A GIRL...

AREN'T YOU LOOKING FOR A BOYFRIEND?
ALTHOUGH I'M NOT LOOKING FOR ONE FOR ME...
OH...
YES...

IF YOU DON'T MIND...
...I CAN INTRODUCE YOU TO ONE OF MY ACQUAIN-TANCES.

WHAT?

ERR...BUT... IT HAS TO BE A MARRIAGE-MINDED RELATIONSHIP...
PERFECT! THAT'S NOT A PROBLEM!!

ARE YOU...
...SURE?

YES!
JUST WAIT A MINUTE!

WOW...
LOOKS LIKE THERE ARE KIND PEOPLE ON EARTH, TOO.
じ〜ん…
I'M SO GLAD... NOW I CAN FINISH MY ASSIGNMENT AND GO BACK TO SIREN.

THANK YOU FOR WAITING!

OH...
WOW

BIG BROTHER! ♡
I HAVE A FRIEND WHO'D LIKE TO MARRY YOU! ♡
ぶりっ♡
SIS, YOU CAME TO THE RIGHT GUY!
I'm happy to be of service!
Hey, aren't you Koyomi? ♡
EEEEK!!
This guy again?!
KOYOMI!
KYAAAAA!!
ぶわっ
WHY DO YOU HATE MEN SO?!
IT'S TRULY TRAGIC.
WHAT? HUH?

MARK MY WORDS!

MAN WAS MADE FOR WOMEN.

HE PROTECTS THEM!

HELPS THEM!

SUPPORTS THEM!!

MAKES THEM HAPPY!!

THAT'S A MAN'S PURPOSE!

IT'S JOYOUS!

DO YOU UNDERSTAND THAT, KOYOMI?

OH...

I THOUGHT THAT ALL MEN WERE SCARY...BUT...

FUKU-YAMA...

I...

SO LET'S MAKE LOVE RIGHT NOW!!
むぎゅ♡
AAAH!!
NOOOOOOO!!!
Squeeze
Waaaaa!..
Excuse me...
KOYOMI?
DID SOMETHING HAPPEN TO YOU?
Something must have happened...
SHE DUG ANOTHER HOLE... WE'D BETTER BE CAREFUL...
BOSS... I CAN'T HANDLE THIS ASSIGNMENT...
OH, MOM... THIS IS A VERY SCARY PLACE...

Act.14 • END

Act.15

ARE YOU TWO LOOKING FOR PART-TIME JOBS?

THANKS TO MIHARU'S FOOD EXPENSES, AND KOYOMI'S LIVING COSTS...

...THE SASAKI FAMILY IS ALMOST BANKRUPT.

SIGN: Kojima

SHE'S RIGHT... SIREN'S MONEY IS USELESS ON EARTH.

WHAT'LL WE DO?

I SEE...

SO THAT'S WHY YOU'RE LOOKING FOR PART-TIME JOBS.

THEN, I KNOW THE PERFECT JOB FOR YOU.

Act.
15

ARE YOU TWO READY?
ガチャ
GOOD. YOU LOOK GREAT!!
ERR...
WHAT KIND OF JOB IS THIS?

WELL, IT'S LIKE BEING A BOOTH BUNNY.
IT'S PLAYING HOSTESS FOR A CHILDREN'S EVENT.

GIVING KIDS QUIZZES FOR STUFFED ANIMALS ON THE STAGE...

GIVING AWAY AWARDS TO KIDS, STUFF LIKE THAT.

OH.
SO WE'RE WORKING WITH KIDS.

THAT'S RIGHT. CAN YOU HANDLE IT, KOYOMI?
SURE I CAN!

OH!
RIGHT. I ALMOST FORGOT...
?
HEY!! COME OVER HERE QUICKLY!
WAUGH!

WE HAVE ANOTHER HELPER TODAY!
Say hi!
HELLO. NICE TO MEET YOU. I'M YUKINA SATOU. ♡
Kya! ♡
PLEASED TO WORK WITH YOU...
...TO... TODAY.
MISS SATOU? HAVE I SEEN YOU SOMEWHERE?
?
WHAT?!
びくぅっ
NO, I THINK THAT THIS IS THE FIRST TIME WE'VE MET...
ドキドキ
Several hours ago...
C'MON, KIRIE...

AREN'T YOU WORRIED ABOUT MIHARU?
IF SO, STOP COMPLAINING AND PUT THEM ON!
ズボッ
AH!
HEY!
AAH!
Kyaaaa!
STOP IT!
ポイ
ポイ
THEY'LL NEVER BUY THIS...
IT'LL WORK BETTER WHEN YOU'RE IN AN AUDIENCE FULL OF CHILDREN.
IN THAT COSTUME, YOU CAN SUPPORT MIHARU FROM RIGHT UP CLOSE!
Is there a problem?
BY THE WAY, YOU LOOK NICE IN IT!
IT'S ONLY THIRTY MINUTES. DEAL WITH IT
Ha ha ha ha ha ha ha!
だぁ～
KIRIE, YOU'RE EVIL...
THIS IS A DISASTER...
HELLO! THANK YOU FOR COMING TODAY!
THE SHOW IS ABOUT TO START!!
HEY, KIDS! HOW ARE YOU TODAY?

I'M FINE, THANKS!!
GO AWAY!
WAAA!
MOMMY!
FUKUYAMA?! WHY ARE YOU HERE?!

"WHY?"
I WANT TO SEE HOW YOUR JOB'S GOING!
I'm also supporting you with this fashionable team sweatshirt!
BUT I DIDN'T KNOW MIHARU AND KOYOMI WORKED HERE, TOO. WELL, I'M GLAD I CAME!

FUKUYAMA SURE CARES ABOUT HIS FRIENDS.
THAT'S CRAP!
He's just being sleazy, as usual!

WELL, WELL. WHY DON'T YOU GET IT STARTED NOW, HOT STUFF!
UGH...

HEH HEH HEH... TODAY...
I'M GOING TO SHOOT...

... MIHARU, KOYOMI AND KOJIMA FROM LOW ANGLES!

!

Click

TODAY WE'RE GIVING AWAY BALLOONS! PLEASE ENJOY THE SHOW!

WE'LL ALSO HAVE THE HAND-SHAKING EVENT WITH KOOKY BEAR AND BAKA BUNNY.

....

HEY!

Alley oop!

What's he up to?!

HEY! WHAT THE HELL ARE YOU DOING?!
GAH!
Eep.

NOTHING GOO-- OH, CRAP.
WAAA WAAA! I'M SCARED!

I...
I'M SORRY.
IT'S BAD MANNERS FOR YOUR HOST TO BEAT UP A GUEST.
HEY, NOW! BIG BOY OVER THERE! ♡
YOU CAN'T TAKE PICTURES WITHOUT ASKING! ♡
Caution: She's working!

!!
OH WELL.
WOW! THIS PLACE IS FUN!
Ha ha ha!
JUST YOU WAIT...

HERE'S A BALLOON FOR YOU.
OVER HERE! OVER HERE!! I WANT A BALLOON TOO!!

HERE!

FOR YOU! ♡

...THANK...
YOU'RE WELCOME.

DON'T EVEN THINK ABOUT GETTING NEAR MIHARU.

WHAT'S YOUR NAME?
YUKINA SATOU! ♡
Hee hee! ♥

YUKINA... THAT'S A CUTE NAME.
YOUR NAME'S NOT THE ONLY THING THAT'S CUTE...
YIKES!
ERR... WELL...
BACK OFF, YOU PERVERT!
YOU SHOULD HAVE FOUND ME SOONER!
I'M ALWAYS READY FOR...
ぐぐ
んぐぐ
OHH...
THAT'S...
Ready for what?!
NO!
I'M SHY!!
GOOOMPH!
KYAAAAA!!
?!
Koyomi?!

WHOA!!
THERE SURE ARE A LOT OF BIG KIDS HERE TODAY!
Pant
THE HOSTESSES FOR THIS EVENT ARE REALLY TOP NOTCH!
CUTE AS CAN BE. ♡
Pant
AAH....
They're hyperventilating.
Creepy!
Pant
THIS'LL BE A GREAT PHOTO SHOOT.
Pant
WOULD YOU POSE ALL TOGETHER?
Pant

KIRIE...
WHO ARE THOSE PEOPLE?
THEY MUST HAVE HEARD ABOUT THIS EVENT SOMEWHERE AND JUST SHOWED UP.
Through the horny guy grapevine!
YOU SAID THIS WAS A CHILDREN'S EVENT...
IF WE DON'T DO SOMETHING, WE WON'T BE ABLE TO FINISH THE SHOW.
わあ
YOU APE!
DON'T PUSH ME!
わあ
THAT HURTS!
YAAAH! PEOPLE ARE...
MIHARU, WATCH OUT!!

AH!
ガッシャン
!!
OOF!
OOH!
OW!
ズズゥン
OWIE...
!
YUKINA?!
...UNH...

YUKINA! ARE YOU OKAY?
HUH?!
AH HA HA HA...
I'M FINE. PERFECTLY FINE!
BUT...
I'M GLAD YOU'RE OKAY...
YEAH...
YOU'RE BLEEDING!
REALLY... DON'T FUSS OVER ME...
OH, BOY. AT THIS RATE, YUKINARI WON'T SURVIVE TO THE END OF THE EVENT.
WOW.
ボソッ
FOXY...

YUKINA SAVED HER CO-WORKER WITHOUT THOUGHT TO HER OWN SAFETY...

AND DESPITE HER INJURY, SHE JUST SMILED AND LAUGHED IT OFF...

Click

FROM WHAT I HEAR, YUKINA **ALWAYS** PROTECTS OTHER GIRLS...

pant

pant

SHE'S TOO HOT!!!

OH, NO.

THIS CAN'T BE GOOD.

ANIMALS!!

DON'T TOUCH MY YUKINA!!

FUKU-YAMA?

FUKUYAMA IS PROTECTING ME?!

MAYBE HE'S NOT SUCH A BAD GUY!

WHAT?! SINCE WHEN WAS SHE YOURS?!

YUKINA'S LOVED BY EVERYBODY!

ABSOLUTELY. THAT'S RIGHT.

SHE BELONGS TO THE WORLD!!

ドタ ドタ ドタ ドタ

ALLOW ME TO HANDLE THIS!

FUKU-YAMA?!

うぉおおおおぉ
ドドドドド
AARGH!!
YUKI-CAKES!
OH, SHIT!
YAAA! FUKUYAMA, YOU'RE USELESS!
ズザァア
HEY, WHAT'S GOING ON?!
NOOOOOOOOOOO!
Huzzah!!
A CELE-BRATION?!
ドキ
IT'S AN ARMY OF MEN!
ドキ
Hurrah!!
Hollah!!

THIS...
THIS IS...
EEP.
...SO NOT GOOD!!
YUKINA! FIGHT BACK!
MIHARU, STOP THAT CHEERING! FIND KOYOMI!
We gotta get outta here!
SHE DUG A HOLE AGAIN!!!
A huge one right on the stage!
SO SCARY... SO MANY MEN...

FLYING BUTT KICK!!!

YAAA!

ドカッ

HYAK!

GAH!

HMPH.

IDIOTS...

FU... FUKUYAMA...?

NOW!!

GIVE THE HERO SOME LOVIN'!

NO GOOD! HE ISN'T LISTENING TO ME AT ALL!!

Waaa!

HEY! STOP!

These clothes aren't mine!

Eek!

STOP IT!! WHERE DO YOU THINK YOU'RE TOUCHING?!

I'LL BUY YOU SOME NEW THREADS, HOT STUFF. ♡

Yaaaah!

WOW! ISN'T THIS MORE EXCITING OUTDOORS? ♡

YOU'D BE EXCITED OVER A FENCE-POST!

EXCUSE ME, BUT SHOULDN'T YOU BE SAVING HER?

OH, SHE'S FINE!!

EH?
YUKINA... YOUR... CHEST IS....
...flat?!
HE FINALLY NOTICED!
HA HA HA!!
I'M SORRY FOR TRICKING...

Sound FX: Squeeze

YOU MORON! IT'S ME! YUKINARI!! CAN'T YOU TELL?!

...HUH?

CHI.. CHIBI... NARI...?
THAT'S RIGHT! IT'S CHIBI-NARI, YOUR ENEMY!!
Now let go!

FUKUYAMA'S GIVEN UP THE GHOST...

OY VEY...
Fuku-yama?!

HUH?
HE GOT YUKINA ALONE...
IT'S NOT FAIR...
YECCH...
IT WAS A HORRIBLE... HORRIBLE...
Chibinari! I'll kill you for this!
AIIIEEE!
KICK HIS BUTT!
HEY!
TAKE THIS!
THE EVENT WAS A DISASTER.
FUKUYAMA WAS HOSPITALIZED FOR MASSIVE BLUNT TRAUMA...
...AND I ALMOST BECAME MALE-PHOBIC, TOO.
SO MUCH FOR GETTING PAID.
WORKING ON THE EARTH IS INSANE...
BY THE WAY, WHERE DID YUKINA GO?
HUNH?
Wah!
Wah!
If we owe the park money, Yukinari's paying for it...

Act.15 • END

Act.16
WE HAD GONE TO A CHRISTMAS PARTY AT THE FUKUYAMA RESIDENCE.
RIGHT.
I'M JUST LOOKING FOR A BATH-ROOM...
WHAT THE...?!
C'MON!
WHAT'S THIS NON-SENSE ROOM?!
AGH!!
OH, NO! I BROKE IT.
WAS IT EXPENSIVE? WHAT SHOULD I DO?

...IS FULL OF STRANGE ARTIFACTS.

AND EVERYTHING LOOKS SUPER EXPENSIVE.

ARE THEY ALL RISA'S THINGS?

AND THIS MIRROR...

THE SURFACE LOOKS LIKE MOVING WATER. STRANGE...

WHAT?!

Act. 16

ゴロン
OOOH...
......?
HUH?
きょろ
きょろ
WHERE AM I?
LAST TIME I CHECKED...
...I WAS AT FUKUYAMA'S HOUSE WITH THE OTHERS.

HELLO, LADIES!
I'M VERY PLEASED THAT YOU CAME! ♡
What's with his costume?
YOU WERE NOT INVITED!
GET OUT!
Aahhh!
YUKI-NARI!
ARROGANT AND MEAN, AS USUAL.
BIG BROTHER!
YOUR PRESENCE IS NOT REQUIRED AT MY PARTY!
Get out of here, now!
FUKUYAMA, PLEASE DON'T BEAT YUKINARI!
I'M SCARED.
YOU'RE HORRIBLE!
Waaa!
SOMETIMES A PUNCH SAYS MORE THAN WORDS!

STOP IT!
HUH?!
AWW...
RISA...
Who needs more guys here?
YUKINARI IS MY VERY SPECIAL GUEST!
WELL, YUKI-NARI.
LET'S BE LOVERS, LIKE FATE INTENDED! ♡
OH!
YEEEP!
TCH... I'LL LET IT SLIDE THIS TIME...
Grit
ANYWAY!
EEP.
Haa...

LET'S ENJOY OUR-SELVES!!
NO!!
ENOUGH IS ENOUGH!!
YOU ARE ALWAYS, ALWAYS, ALWAYS--!!
......
OUCH!
AND SO...
...I WENT TO THE BATHROOM.

BUT...
...WHILE ROAMING THIS HUGE MANSION...
...I ENDED UP IN THIS ROOM BY MISTAKE.

THEN, I BROKE THIS VASE.

HUH? IT'S NOT BROKEN?

HMM. THIS MIRROR WAS...?

OH!

OH MY!

ISN'T THAT...

...THE VASE I BROKE?!

DOES THAT MEAN...

HERE IS...

...INSIDE THE MIRROR?!

NO!!

I'VE GOTTA GET OUT OF HERE!

THERE MUST BE AN EXIT SOMEWHERE!

I HAVE TO FIND IT!

OH!

WHAT THE...?
FUKU-YAMA?
AIIIEEEEEE!!

WH...
WHAT'S WRONG?
DON'T SHOUT FOR NO REASON.

YIKES...
WHY ARE YOU RUNNING AWAY?

HEY! HOW DO I GET OUT OF THIS WEIRD--
DON'T COME ANY CLOSER! I'LL DIE!

あう
DON'T YOU KNOW HOW MUCH I HATE WOMEN?!
PLEASE GO AWAY! WAUGH!
ああああああ

?
HATE... WOMEN?!
What are you talking about?!

HERE!
HELL-LO!!
BOOBS?!
YOU KNOW, BOOBS?! WHAT DO YOU SAY?!
AIIIIEEEE!
STOP IT!
THEY'RE MAKING ME SICK!
Hyunk
HOW RUDE!
OOG.
WHERE'S THE HORNY FUKUYAMA?!
Lemme 'lone!
I can still see you!
OH!
FUKUYAMA! THERE YOU ARE!

I CAUGHT YOU! ♡
JEEZ! KOYOMI?!
?!
NOW!
LET'S MAKE LOVE! ♡
NO WAY!
Leave me alone!
WHY NOT?!

ALL MY SEARCHING WAS WORTH IT...
...TO HAVE MET A WONDERFUL MAN LIKE YOU!
THIS...IS MY FIRST TIME, BUT I'LL DO MY BEST!
Kiii!!
BEST?
BEST WHAT?!

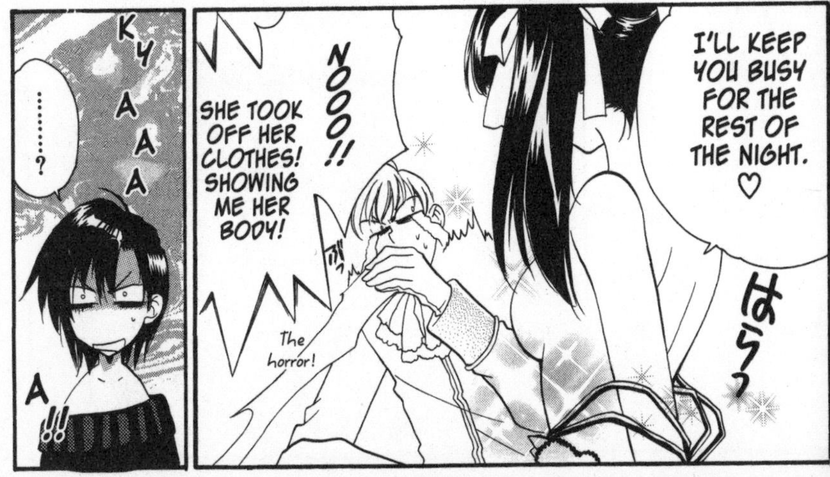

AB...
I HAD TO GET OUT. WHAT'S WITH FUKUYAMA?
ABNORMAL!

FUKUYAMA HATES WOMEN AND...
...KOYOMI LOVES MEN?!

IT'S COMPLETELY OPPOSITE OF WHAT'S NORMAL.
IT'S CRAZY! CRAZY!!
JUST BECAUSE THIS IS A WORLD INSIDE A MIRROR--

MIRROR?!

IS IT POSSIBLE?
IS EVERYBODY OPPOSITE BECAUSE IT'S A REFLECTION?

THEN...
What do I do now?
KIRIE!!

YU...
YUKINARI?

?
YEAH? WHAT'S THE MATTER? YOU LOOK LIKE YOU 'ON'T TRUST ME.

ARE YOU REALLY YUKINARI?
OF COURSE I'M YUKINARI.

ARE YOU REALLY THE REAL YUKINARI?

YES, IT'S ME. YOUR CHILDHOOD PAL, YUKINARI SASAKI!

GOOD!
I THOUGHT YOU'D BE WEI--
?!

pant
pant
KIRIE, I WANT YOU!!
WHAAAT?!
H- HEY!
I'M GOING TO KICK YOUR BUTT IF YOU DON'T STOP MESSING AROUND!
STOP IT!
I'M NOT JOKING!
WHA?
I'VE WANTED YOU SINCE I WAS LITTLE.
YIKES!

HEY...
STOP TEARING OFF MY CLOTHES!!
FIRST OF ALL, YOU'RE ALLERGIC TO WOMEN!
IF YOU TOUCH ME...
UGH
DAMMIT! IT'S THE MIRROR YUKINARI!!
OWW!
No!!
STOP!!
!
Yaaah!

"The Exorcizer"
SEDUCER!!! BEGONE, I SAY!
GAAH!
EEEEK!!
AHHHH... RI...RISA?
へたり
どっ
ANOTHER MIRROR PERSON...
BUT WHAT'S RISA LIKE IN THIS WORLD?! SHE STILL SEEMS TO BE INTO THE OCCULT...
......

OH, KIRIE! I'M SO GLAD YOU'RE OKAY! ♡
Ha ha ha!
OH, I'M ALL RIGHT!!
YOU AND I ARE BOUND BY A LOVE THAT ONLY TWO WOMEN CAN UNDERSTAND. ♡
WAIT A SECOND!
THIS ISN'T MY KIND OF THING!

UH, RISA?!
どさっ
WOW...
YOUR BOOBS ARE BIG! ♡
I'M EMBARRASSED TO BE SO INADEQUATE FOR YOU. ♡
BUT SINCE WE'RE BOTH GIRLS...
...THERE'S NOTHING TO BE SHY ABOUT, RIGHT?
OH, KIRIE...
KOJIMA! HELP ME!!
YIKES!
THAT'S RIGHT!
THERE'S NOTHING TO BE SHY ABOUT!!
Sigh...
YAAAA!
AAAAAAAA!

NOOOO OOO OOOO!!!

I CAN'T TAKE THIS PLACE!!

Kirie?!

Big sister?!

WAAAA

KIRIE!
WHAT HAPPENED TO YOU?
MIHARU, HELP ME!
I CAN'T GO THROUGH FROM THIS SIDE!
PLEASE! PULL ME FROM YOUR SIDE!!
MIHARU?!
BIG SISTER!
KIRIE!
KOJIMA!

GACK!

LEAVE ME THE HELL ALONE!

I DON'T BELONG ON THIS SIDE OF THE MIRROR!

OOF!

OOH...
OH MY!

...I ...
What's going on here?
I'M SAVED!
What happened to you, Kojima?

HUH?
WHAT?

にゅっ

BIG SISTER! ♡

OUCH!

?!!

ズル

WHAT THE?!

They're following me?!

?

N... NOOOO!!!
THEY TOLD ME IT TOOK THREE DAYS AND NIGHTS TO PUT THEM BACK THROUGH THE MIRROR.

Act.16 • END

Act.17

♪ ♪

THE MONEY I EARNED FROM MY FORMER PART-TIME JOB...

GIFTS FOR THE FRIENDS I MADE THIS YEAR...

WHAT SHOULD I CHOOSE? I HAVE TO FIND SOMETHING THEY'D LIKE.

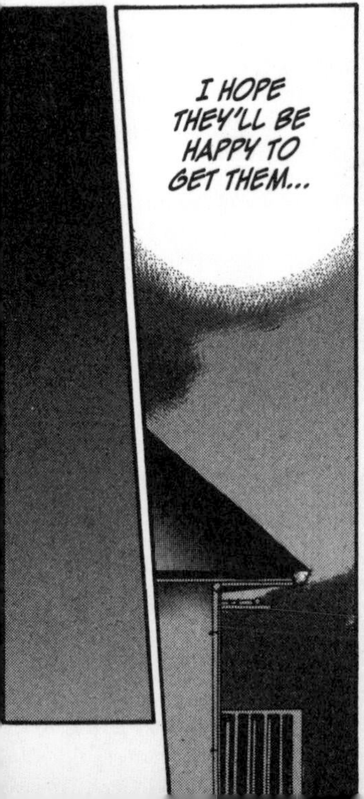

Act.
17

HA HA! ♡
YEAR END SUPER SALE
FOR KIRIE.
FOR KOYOMI.
FOR RISA.
FOR FUKUYAMA.
AND FOR YUKINARI!
I GOT GIFTS FOR EVERYONE! ♡
Tap
Tap

ALL I HAVE TO DO NOW IS GIVE THEM THE GIFTS.

BUT HOW SHOULD I DO IT??

!

KIRIE!
IS THAT...
...MIHARU'S VOICE?

JUST THE PERSON I WANTED TO SEE!
IN FACT, I HAVE SOMETHING THAT I'D LIKE TO HAND TO YOU.
OH... ERR...

I'M JUST ABOUT TO GO OUT.
KOJIMA!!

I'M HERE TO SEE YOU, AS PROMISED.
KIRIE?
THAT'S UNUSUAL...
ARE YOU GOING OUT WITH RISA?
HUH?
NO...
...IT ISN'T.
RISA AND I ARE VERY CLOSE! ♡
O-OF COURSE, BIG SISTER!
Right?!
SO, WE HAVE TO GO!!
SEE YA LATER, MIHARU!!
W...
WAIT A SECOND!
I HAVE SOMETHING FOR YOU!
AND ALSO RISA...
ER...

MIHARU, A MOOCH LIKE YOU, WHO'S ONLY GOOD FOR HOUSE-KEEPING...

...WOULD DO BETTER FOR YUKINARI IF YOU JUST STAYED AT HOME.

!

KOJIMA TOLD ME SHE CAN'T STAND HANGING AROUND WITH YOU!

WELL, G'BYE.

Ha ha ha!

...I...

DIDN'T KNOW THEY THOUGHT OF ME LIKE THAT. AND WHAT'S A MOOCH?

!

KOYOMI?
OH...
KOYOMI, ARE YOU GOING OUT, TOO?
ERR...UH... I'M NOT....
...SNEAKING OUT OF THE HOUSE WHILE YOU WERE AWAY...
NOPE, NOT ME!!
Ahhh!
Ahhh!
WAAA!!
I'M ABOUT TO GO TO WORK! YEAH, WORK!
KOYOMI, THAT WAS THE SADDEST EXCUSE FOR A LIE I'VE EVER HEARD!
Ah! I can't do this any more!
KOYOMI, DO YOU DISLIKE ME, TOO?
IS THAT IT?
NO...
Waaa!
Waaa!
THAT'S NOT IT! I'M JUST TRYING TO MAKE YOU BELIEVE... THAT... UMM...

W... WHY...
...IS EVERYONE SUDDENLY AVOIDING ME?
WHY?!!
WHOA!! WHAT'S WRONG WITH YOU, MIHARU?!
Sniff...
Sniff...
KO... KOYOMI...
SHE MUST BE ANGRY WITH ME BECAUSE I USED UP HER POINTS FROM HER FIRST MISSION...
THAT HAS TO BE IT...
THAT **HAS** TO BE IT...

Sniff...
Sniff...
ポタッ
タッ...
HIC.
ゴシ
ゴシ

THEY'LL BE GLAD TO GET THEM, RIGHT?
THEN WILL THEY STOP AVOIDING ME?

ALSO...
...I CAN DO IT...
...I WON'T EAT SO MUCH...
...JUST A LITTLE BIT...
...NO...AS LITTLE AS POSSIBLE...
I'M HOME!

YUKINARI!
YUKINARI.
I... I'M...
MIHARU.
I'M SORRY TO ASK THIS SO SUDDENLY...

COULD YOU GO OUT AND KILL SOME TIME FOR A WHILE?

ぽろ

ぽろ

EVEN...

...YUKINARI DISLIKES ME!

とっぷり...

MIHARU IS LATE...

YOU'RE RIGHT.

SO'S MY BROTHER.

HE WENT OUT TO GET SOME DRINKS AND HASN'T COME BACK YET.

Happy New Year's Eve
Thank you, Miharu!
AND WE FINALLY FINISHED EVERYTHING FOR THE PARTY, TOO...
I KNOW...
I'M GETTING WORRIED.
I'M GOING TO LOOK FOR HER!!
IF YUKINARI'S GOING, SO AM I.
I'VE GOT A BAD FEELING...

SIGH...

WHERE HAS MIHARU GONE?

SHE WAS EATING EVERYTHING ON THAT TABLE.
SHE MIGHT EVEN EAT THE TABLE.
HOW CAN SOMEONE SO SKINNY PUT SO MUCH FOOD INTO HER BODY?
DON'T...
...TELL ME...

EH?
DUDE, WASN'T THAT GIRL AMAZING?
YEAH.

IT HAS TO BE!
Miharu!!
?!

KEEP IT COMIN'!!
More!
HEY. HURRY UP!
Bring some meat!
THERE'S STILL MORE ROOM IN HER STOMACH!
I'll cover her tab!

Great. She's drunk, Fukuyama's here and she's multiplied.
SNIFF! FUKUYAMA! YUKINARI IS... KIRIE IS... RISA IS... KOYOMI IS...
MIHARU!
JUST TAKE OFF YOUR CLOTHES, AND I'LL CURE YOUR BROKEN HEART!

※ Miharu multiplies herself out of paranoia when she's drunk (See Volume 2, Act 8).

DON'T TRY TO TAKE ADVANTAGE...
...OF MIHARU BEING WASTED!
?!
THEN WHAT SHOULD I DO?!
HOW ABOUT NOTHING?!
BUT THAT'S IMPOSSIBLE!
HA HA HA HA!!
Fukuyama
oks funny!

Hic.
HEY DUDE, TELL ME!
DO YOU EVER GET TIRED OF LIFE'S HARDSHIPS?
SURE!! I CAN'T COPE WITHOUT DRINKING! DRINK THIS!!
Drink up!
HEY! DON'T GIVE HER MORE BOOZE!
NOOOO!!

YUKINARI, YOU'RE A JERK!!

WHY ME?!

No!

YUKI-NARI!

JERK! JERK! JERK!! JERK!!!

Yow!

ALTHOUGH I CONSTANTLY EAT EVERYTHING IN YOUR HOUSE...

...IT'S TERRIBLE OF YOU TO KICK ME OUT FOR IT!!

NOBODY DISLIKES YOU.
ALL OF US CAME TO LOOK FOR YOU BECAUSE WE'RE WORRIED.
COME ON...
LET'S GO HOME NOW.

IS IT...
...TRUE?
NOBODY HATES ME?

A LOT OF FUN THINGS HAPPEN WHEN YOU'RE AROUND, MIHARU!
THERE'S NO WAY WE'D DISLIKE YOU!

IT'S TRUE! WE'VE BEEN LOOKING FOR YOU EVERYWHERE.
REALLY!
Tch.

ISN'T THAT RIGHT, GUYS?

I DON'T KNOW QUITE HOW TO PUT THIS...
...BUT I ENJOY HAVING YOU STAY AT MY HOUSE.

ME, TOO...ERR... THANKS TO MIHARU, I CAME TO THE EARTH...
...AND I MET KIRIE, RISA AND YUKINARI...

KOYOMI, YOU'VE FOR-GOTTEN ME!

AS FOR YOU, YOU'VE MADE YOUR FIRST MALE FRIEND SINCE YOUR BIRTH.
WHO--
WHO'S MY FRIEND?!
No!!

I DON'T REMEMBER EVER BECOMING YOUR FRIEND!
I DON'T WANT A FRIEND LIKE YOU!

HEY!
RISA!
....

I DIDN'T REALLY WANT TO SAY THIS, BUT...
Squeeze
IF YOU HADN'T COME TO EARTH OR TO YUKINARI'S PLACE...
...THE WHEEL OF FATE WOULD HAVE NEVER LET ME MEET YUKINARI...

I ACCEPT YOU!
ONLY FOR TODAY!!
UNWILL-INGLY!
RISA...

BUT REMEMBER, IT'S ONLY FOR TODAY!
JUST ONE DAY!!
DO YOU GET IT?!
She's overcompen-sating...
ALL YOU GUYS...
THANK YOU VERY MUCH.

I'M SORRY FOR...
...MAKING YOU WORRY.
I'M ALSO...
...VERY PLEASED TO HAVE MET YOU ALL.
I LOVE YOU ALL!

AND SO...

HERE'S TO THE NEW YEAR! ♡

ct.17 • END

Act.18

MIHARU! KOYOMI!

WHAT, KIRIE?

WHAT DID YOU BUY?

Note: Setsubun is a holiday for wishing for good luck and getting rid of bad luck by tossing roasted soybeans.

WE LIVE IN JAPAN!
DON'T YOU WANT OUR SIRENESE GUESTS TO EXPERIENCE THE GOOD LUCK RITUAL?
GOOD LUCK?
OH! I REMEMBER!

Act. 18

LIKE THIS, KIRIE?

YEP.

KEEP ROASTING THEM LIKE THAT FOR A WHILE!

OKAY!

Sizzle

NEXT, GRAB THE ROASTED BEANS.

AND FROM INSIDE OF THE HOUSE, SHOUT, "BAD SPIRITS OUT! GOOD SPIRITS IN!"

Like this.

SAY THAT, THEN TOSS THEM OUT.

WHAT DO YOU THINK?
ISN'T IT EASY AND FUN?
REALLY... TO GET RID OF BAD SPIRITS LIKE THIS...
ISN'T IT FASCINATING, MIHARU?
BUT...
I FEEL KIND OF SORRY...
...ABOUT KEEPING THE BAD SPIRITS OUT OF THE HOUSE.
ACTUALLY, MIHARU, "BAD SPIRITS" ARE A METAPHOR. IT'S MORE LIKE KEEPING THE BAD THINGS IN THE WORLD OUT OF THE HOUSE.
THAT'S RIGHT!
FOR GOOD LUCK!
?!

GIRLS COME IN!! ♡
GUYS GET OUT!!
THAT'S HOW YOU DO IT.
NO, IT ISN'T!
THE RITUAL IS ALSO TO RID THE WORLD OF GARBAGE* AND MY ENEMIES**!
Ha ha ha!
IS IT REALLY?
ふふふふ…
*Men **Men
?!
HEY, YUKINARI!
TOSS OUT THIS TRESPASSER!
He's ruining the ritual!

ANOTHER CRASHER!
YUKINARI, PLEASE EAT RISA'S SPECIAL BEANS. ♡
Ha ha ha!
THEY'RE GUARANTEED TO GIVE YOU PERFECT HEALTH. ♡
KI-KIRIEE... HELP ME...

AND NOW WE'RE BACK TO THE REGULAR STORYLINE!
♡ YUMMY, YUMMY BEANS FOR YOU!! ♡
Taste them!
N-NO! THEY MUST BE HEXED!!
Don't touch me!

FORGET THEM. LET'S TOSS BEANS OVER HERE!
LET ME SEE...
WHO'S GOING TO PLAY THE BAD SPIRIT?
!!

I'VE ALREADY TAKEN CARE OF THAT!

I INVITED SOME REAL SPIRITS!

I'M KIKI.

I'M RARA.

AAAAH!

YIKES!

NO!!

ABSOLUTELY NOT!!!

Send them away now!

I JUST WANTED TO ENJOY THE RITUAL WITH YUKINARI MORE REALISTICALLY...
THIS ISN'T ABOUT REALISM!
HEY!
CHIBINARI! DON'T GROPE MY LITTLE SISTER!!!

WHAT? ARE YOU BLIND?!
She's the molester!
WHAT?!
WHOEVER TOLD YOU YOU'VE GOT THE BALLS TO TALK BACK TO ME?!
This is about beans, not balls!
I WON'T HAVE THIS!

CHIBINARI, OUT!!
HEY!
THOSE ARE MIHARU'S BEANS!
OUCH!
........?

OH!
AH!
WA!
OH!
AH!
HUH?
YOW!

......!?
YUKI-NARI?

THAT'S RIGHT! NO MATTER HOW MUCH YOU HATE YUKINARI...

...YOU'VE GONE TOO FAR!!

OH...

しゅっ

BIG BROTHER, YOU SHOULD LEAVE!!

?!

OH!
HA!
HUH?
AAH!
AAH!
ARRGH!!
SIGH
YUKINARI'S HURT AGAIN!!
HA HA HA!
THAT'S FOR BULLYING YUKINARI.
Hey!
BY THE WAY...

WHAT THE HECK IS GOING ON?!
MAYBE RISA CAN, BUT FUKU-YAMA CAN'T DO WEIRD TRICKS...

EXCUSE ME...

THOSE BEANS THAT KAZUHARU AND RISA USED...
THEY WERE THE ONES MIHARU PREPARED EARLIER.
COULD THE BEANS BE THE CAUSE?

HEY, MIHARU...
...DID YOU DO ANYTHING WHILE YOU WERE ROASTING BEANS??
HUH?

NO...
...I JUST ASKED THEM TO REMOVE BAD THINGS.

......
THAT'S IT!

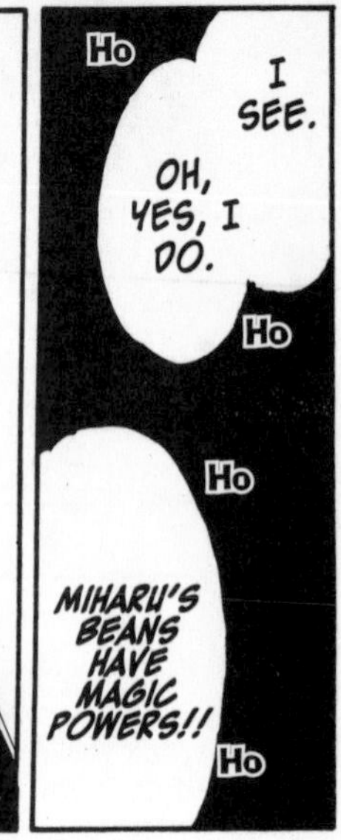
Ho
I SEE.
OH, YES, I DO.
Ho
Ho
MIHARU'S BEANS HAVE MAGIC POWERS!!
Ho

Got my mojo working!
THEN, I'M GOING TO REMOVE CHIBINARI FROM THIS HOUSE!!
HA HA!
HA HA
HA HA HA HA HA HA HA HA!!

CHIBINARI, GET...

...OUT!!!
YAAGH!

OUT!
OUT!
PTOO!
OU--
What?!

STOP IT!!

OWW!!

FUKUYAMA, YOU DUMBASS!

ARE YOU GOING TO KILL YOUR ONLY FRIEND?!

Huh?!

Gaa!

LIKE I SAID BEFORE, *WE'RE NOT FRIENDS!!*

YUKINARI. I'M SORRY...

BECAUSE... I...I... MADE THOSE BEANS...

NO...

IT'S FUKUYAMA'S FAULT. YOU DIDN'T DO ANYTHING WRONG.

HAA!

MIHARU, GET OUT!!
Take that!
There!
HEY HEY HEY!!
?!
RISA! DON'T BANISH MIHARU!
THAT'S A NO-NO!
TCH.
Start-ling!
EEEEK!!
WHY ARE YOU GETTING IN MY WAY?!
You're terrible!!
BIG BROTHER, DO YOU HATE ME?
IS THAT IT?!

THAT'S NOT IT!
I LOVE YOU MORE THAN ANYTHING, RISA!
BUT...I... DESPISE MEN... AND THE XY CHROMOSOME SO MUCH THAT...
I WANT TO RID THE WORLD OF MEN!

THEN WHAT ABOUT THE MAN OF MY DESTINY?!
MADAM MABANYA TOLD ME THAT YUKINARI AND I ARE FATED LOVERS!
SCREW MADAM MABANYA!
I won't have you seeing a madam!
THE EXTERMINATION OF MEN WAS OUR FATHER'S DYING WISH!!
BUT OUR FATHER'S ALIVE!
OOPS.

ANYWAY!!
Ha
ha ha!
GIRLS COME IN!!
Moron.
I CAN'T STAND ANY MEN EXCEPT MYSE--
HUH?

OH! HERE THEY COME!! ♡
What's this?
Eeeek!
Where am I?
YAAGH! THEY REALLY CAME!!
Yikes!

ALL WOMEN...
GET OUT!!
KYAAAAA!!
ドドドド
DAMN... FUKUYAMA...
Yecch.
HE KNOWS ABOUT MY FEMALE-ALLERGY...
HOW CRUEL!
WELL...
TWO CAN PLAY THAT GAME!
MEN COME IN!!
HUH?
WHAT?!

AIEEE!! GUYS!!!
Huh?
What?
Huh?
What's all this, then?!
Ouch! Hey!
NOOO!! TOO MANY MEN!!

IDIOT!!
WHY ME?!

I DON'T CARE ABOUT FUKUYAMA.
BUT KOYOMI'S HERE, TOO!!
Kya!
Uwaaa!
THINK FOR ONCE!

OH...
THAT'S RIGHT ...

UH...
I'M SORRY, KOYOMI.
What'll I do?!
OH...
I CAN'T TELL RIGHT FROM LEFT.
ドタンバタン

OH...
I...I'M...
Waa! Mommy!!
...GOING MAD!
I'LL SAVE YOU, KO-YOMI!
MEN, PLEASE GET OUT!
OH!
MIHARU?
AH!
MIHARU!

EEEEEEEEEEEEK!!!!

ERR...

GUYS...

Eeeeek!

THERE'S A HOLE OUT HERE?!

HEY, RISA! KIKI AND RARA ARE LOOSE--

YUKINARI! WHERE ARE YOU?!

OH! I'M SORRY, YUKINARI.

Boo!

ドカッ

UGH!

LET'S TOSS SOME BEANS... PROPERLY.

OH-HO NO!

ぶる

I just wanted to show our guests our rituals...

ぶる

DIDN'T YOU GUYS START ALL OF THIS?

ぶる

BOTH OF YOU...

...GET OUT AND THINK ABOUT WHAT YOU'VE DONE!

?!

NOW! LET'S EAT A BEAN FOR EVERY YEAR WE'VE BEEN ALIVE.
YEAH!
....
MY BROTHER'S AN IDIOT!!
Please let us in!

Act.18 • END

Act.19

YAHOO!

WHAT A LOT OF SNOW!

だっ

だっ

I WISH IT SNOWED EVERY DAY.

MOMMY!

......?
ヒュ
ウ
MOMMY?
WHERE ARE YOU?
ぽすっ

Act. 19

どーん!
FINISH-ED!
pant
pant
pant
WOW! THAT'S GREAT! ♡
It's so cute!
REALLY... THAT'S A WONDERFUL SNOWMAN!
YUKINARI! LET'S MAKE A SNOW RABBIT NEXT.
THEN LET'S THROW SNOWBALLS AND...AND...
YEESH!
PLEASE LET ME GET SOME REST...
I'm out of energy...
I'M GOING TO MAKE SOME HOT TEA. LET'S TAKE A BREAK.
It's cold out.
?!

HELLO.

DID YOU COME TO SEE THE SNOWMAN?

......

I CAN'T FIND MY MOMMY.
I CAN'T GO HOME.
ARE YOU LOST?
......
YES.
KOYOMI, WHAT'S GOING ON?

THIS LITTLE GIRL GOT SEPARATED FROM HER MOTHER. SHE SEEMS TO BE LOST.
OH MY. POOR THING...
WHAT'S YOUR NAME?
...KOHARU...
WHERE DID YOU LOSE YOUR MOMMY?
I DON'T KNOW...
WHERE IS YOUR HOME?
I DON'T KNOW ...
...IS THERE ANYTHING YOU REMEMBER?
NO...

NO!

ERR...

I'D LIKE TO DO THIS ALONE, TO GET MORE EXPERIENCE FOR MY JOB.

WELL, IF YOU INSIST.

YES. LET'S LEAVE IT UP TO HER.

Okay?

She'll gain experience points!

THANKS, GUYS.

NOW!
SHALL WE GO?
HUH?
KOHARU, YOU'RE WEARING ONLY ONE GLOVE.
YOU MUST BE COLD. YOU CAN USE MINE!
...NO THANK YOU...
OH... OKAY...
Hmmm...

OH!

すた

すた

HMM... DO YOU REMEMBER ANYTHING LIKE A BUILDING OR PEOPLE?

NO...

YOU *DO* LIVE AROUND HERE, RIGHT, KOHARU?

THEN, YOU MUST HAVE SEEN SOMETHING AROUND HERE...

NO...

NO...

I DON'T KNOW!

ALL I KNOW IS MY MOMMY...

OH!

I'M SORRY. PLEASE DON'T CRY.

WHAT CAN I DO?

UH...

UM...

YOU KNOW...
FINDING PEOPLE IS MY JOB!
SO I'LL DEFINITELY FIND YOUR MOM!

ホッ
SHE STOPPED CRYING.
...AL-THOUGH...
Ha ha ha.
...I HAVE LIMITED EXPER-IENCE...
...AND DON'T ALWAYS GET THE RESULTS I WANT.
....

LET'S START WITH INTER-VIEWING!
THAT'S STEP ONE FOR PEOPLE SEARCHING!!

がた
がた
がた

WHEW...
I'M GETTING TIRED...
Sigh...
BUT I HAVE TO KEEP TRYING...

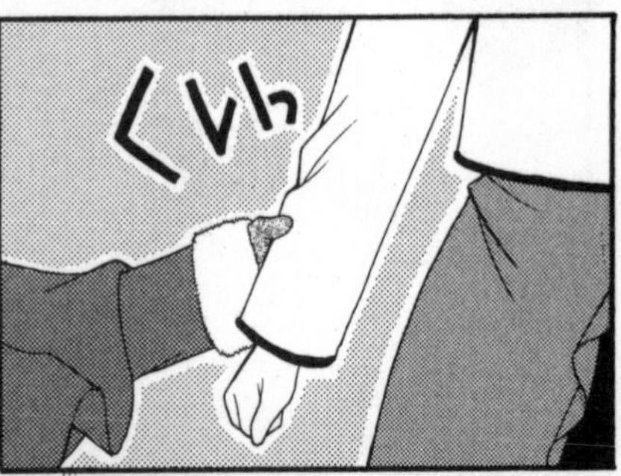

WHAT IS IT?

SIGH...

どよん...

BUT THERE ARE STILL NO CLUES...

HOW MEAN.
SOMEONE KNOCKED OVER THAT SNOWMAN'S MOTHER...
....

BIG SISTER.
LET'S GO BACK.
HUH?
BUT WE HAVEN'T FOUND YOUR MOMMY.
THAT'S FINE!
WE CAN'T FIND MY MOMMY ANYWAY...
ポロ…
KOHARU?
I GET IT.
THEN, SHALL WE GO BACK TO YUKINARI'S HOUSE?
MAYBE YOUR MOMMY OR THE POLICE ARE THERE LOOKING FOR YOU.
......
C'MON.
LET'S GO!
......

THAT'S OKAY.
ALL OF US CAN LOOK FOR HER TOMORROW!!
Right?
THAT'S RIGHT!
ALL OF US WILL LOOK FOR HER TOMORROW.
...NO...
?
WE HAVE TO FIND HER TODAY...

A CHILD IS LONELY WHEN APART FROM THEIR MOTHER...
THE SADNESS I FELT WHEN I LEARNED THAT I WOULD NEVER SEE HER AGAIN...
I DON'T WANT ANYONE ELSE TO FEEL THAT...
SO...
WE DEFINITELY HAVE TO FIND HER TODAY!!

NO ONE...
...ELSE ...

KOYOMI...

BIG SISTER... PLEASE DON'T WORRY. I'M FINE...
NO!
I'M GOING OUT AGAIN TO LOOK FOR HER!

huff
huff
THEN, WHAT SHOULD WE DO?
LET'S EACH SEARCH THREE DIFFERENT AR...

?!

KOYOMI?!

KOYOMI...
OH MY. SHE HAS A FEVER...
FEVER?!
DO WE HAVE ICE PACKS HERE?
LET'S TAKE HER TO HER ROOM FIRST!

...FEVER...?
BIG SISTER KOYOMI...

BIG SISTER...
I'M SORRY...

I KNOW...
...I CAN'T SEE MY MOMMY...
I'M REALLY SORRY...
...FOR SENDING YOU TO FIND HER...

BUT THANK YOU. I WAS VERY HAPPY...
...BECAUSE YOU TRIED SO HARD.

NOW...
IT'S MY TURN...

sizzle
OH...!

OOOH...

KOHARU...
!

TOMORROW...
I...WILL FIND...YOUR MOMMY...

KOYOMI?

YOU WILL.
NOT TOMORROW...

...BUT NEXT YEAR!

HMM...

KO...
...HARU?

ぼーっ…

...I CAN'T GO HOME.
OH...
KOHARU, YOU'RE WEARING ONLY ONE GLOVE.
HOW MEAN.
SOMEONE KNOCKED DOWN THE SNOWMAN'S MOTHER...
I GET IT...
TODAY ...
...WE CAN'T FIND MY MOMMY ANYWAY...

HUH?

WHY'S THIS THING IN THE FREEZER?

YOU'LL FIND OUT EVENTUALLY.

SEE YOU AGAIN...

...WHEN IT SNOWS NEXT YEAR!

OH!

OH!

THAT'S NOT FOR EATING!!

NO!!

?

Act.19 • END

In the next volume of

Spring Flings

You'd expect Miharu and Koyomi to look like a couple of April Fools trying to sort out more strange Earth holidays, but why does Fukuyama think the Easter Bunny hides underwear in the backyard?

Fukuyama's belief might have something to do with Kirie's confusion between bunnies and cat burglars...though it could all be a dream to distract herself from the fact she's suddenly sleeping with Fukuyama!

While Koyomi tries to strike a blow against sexual harassment with her tennis racket, Yukinari tries not to be blown off when another visitor from Siren arrives who completely captures Miharu's--and Risa's--affections.

See you next volume!

GIRLS BRAVO™

THE MANGA THAT INSPIRED THE HIT ANIME!

4

MARIO

"It's Eye-Candy At Its Best"
-AnimeOnDVD.com
GIRLS BRAVO
When fantasy becomes more than you can handle...
Collect The Entire Series!
GENEON
www.GirlsBravoDVD.com
© KANEDA MARIO • KADOKAWA SHOTEN PUBLISHING Co., Ltd. / "GIRLS BRAVO" Production Committee

LIFE

BY KEIKO SUENOBU

Ordinary high school teenagers...
Except that they're not.

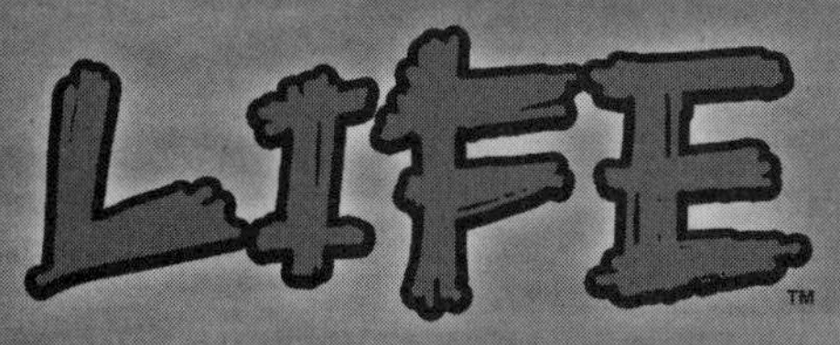

READ THE ENTIRE FIRST CHAPTER ONLINE FOR FREE:

STOP!

This is the back of the book. You wouldn't want to spoil a great ending!

This book is printed "manga-style," in the authentic Japanese right-to-left format. Since none of the artwork has been flipped or altered, readers get to experience the story just as the creator intended. You've been asking for it, so TOKYOPOP® delivered: authentic, hot-off-the-press, and far more fun!

DIRECTIONS

If this is your first time reading manga-style, here's a quick guide to help you understand how it works.

It's easy... just start in the top right panel and follow the numbers. Have fun, and look for more 100% authentic manga from TOKYOPOP®!